The Essential MEXICAN COOKBOOK

50 CLASSIC RECIPES, WITH STEP-BY-STEP PHOTOGRAPHS

EDITED BY

HEATHER THOMAS

COURAGE BOOKS

AN IMPRINT OF RUNNING PRESS
PHILADELPHIA • LONDON

Library of Congress Cataloging-in-Publication Number 94-80086

ISBN 1-56138-599-9

Designed and produced by SP Creative Design
Editor and writer: Heather Thomas
Art director: Al Rockall
Designer: Rolando Ugolini
Special photography: Graham Kirk
Step-by-step photography: GGS Photographics, Norwich
Food preparation: Gillian MacLaurin and Dawn Stock
Styling: Helen Payne
Mexican dishes: Graciella Sanchez and Mexicolore
Produced by Mandarin Offset
Printed and bound in Hong Kong

Published by Courage Books, an imprint of
Running Press Book Publishers
125 South Twenty-second Street
Philadelphia, PA 19103-4399

Notes

1. Standard spoon measurements are used in all recipes.
1 tablespoon = one 15 ml spoon
1 teaspoon = one 5 ml spoon

2. Eggs should be medium unless otherwise stated.

3. Milk should be whole unless otherwise stated.

4. Fresh herbs should be used unless otherwise stated. If
unavailable, use dried herbs as an alternative.
1 tablespoon fresh herbs = 1 teaspoon dried herbs

5. Ovens should be preheated to the specified temperature. If
using a convection oven, follow the manufacturer's instructions
for adjusting the time and temperature.

CONTENTS

INTRODUCTION

Mexican cooking is one of the world's oldest cuisines, interweaving the age-old traditions of the Aztecs with the ingredients and cooking methods introduced by the Spanish conquistadors over 400 years ago. In fact, many of the foods that we take for granted originated in Mexico and were first cultivated there thousands of years ago. The explorers of the New World brought back to Europe vivid tomatoes and sweet peppers, fiery chiles, creamy avocados, colorful beans, aromatic vanilla, exotic guavas and papayas, and chocolate, which was eaten at Montezuma's court. These new culinary discoveries were to change the character and flavors of European and Mediterranean cooking.

Mexican dishes are unique and distinctive— quite unlike the cooking of other countries and cultures. Corn has always been the single most important ingredient and is still the mainstay of Mexican cooks. Tortillas are still made from corn in the traditional way, patted and shaped by hand and cooked on a hot *comal* (griddle) before being fried as *totopos* (tortilla chips), filled with beans, meat, fish, vegetables or cheese, or just served hot as an accompaniment to every meal. However, corn tortillas are often perceived as being rather heavy to our Western palates, and white wheat flour tortillas are now popular.

Avocados

Known to the Aztecs as ahuacatl, avocados have been cultivated in Mexico since 7000BC. They may be rough or smooth skinned and range in color from green to black. Inside, the delicious flesh is pale green with a creamy, buttery texture. They form the basis of guacamole, the classic avocado sauce which is served with literally everything in Mexico.

Avocados are ripe when they yield slightly when pressed with the fingers. Unripe ones will feel hard and should be placed in a paper bag and left for a few days at room temperature to ripen. Avocados discolor rapidly when they are cut, but brushing with lime or lemon juice will help prevent this.

Beans

These originated in Mexico around 5000BC and have remained a staple of Mexican cooking. Many varieties are used: black, navy, kidney and pinto beans are all popular, as are garbanzos which were introduced by the Spanish. The most common way of serving beans is *frijoles refritos* (refried beans). These are beans which have been cooked and are then mashed and fried. The heavy bean paste is used as a filling for tortillas or served with a meal.

Dried beans are soaked in cold water before using, often overnight, until they swell. They are then drained and cooked in fresh water by boiling for two to three hours in an earthenware pot. It is important that they are checked regularly so that they do not boil dry.

Chiles

The colorful chile gives Mexican food its flair and fire. Grown in Mexico for 9,000 years, chiles come in many varieties, fresh and dried. The Mexicans are connoisseurs and regard chiles with the same reverence that the French reserve for their wines. Aficionados can distinguish subtle differences in their

flavor, degree of hotness and intensity. Although we cannot obtain the wide range of chiles that is available in Mexico, the following ones can be purchased in the United States.

Fresh chiles

Jalapeño: these are dark green, long, hot and fiery.

Poblano: these are dark green and tapering and as large as a green pepper. They are often stuffed.

Serrano: these small chiles may be green or red. Hot and tapering, they are used for making guacamole.

Note: take care when handling fresh or dried chiles – the seeds can burn your

skin. Wash your hands thoroughly afterwards or wear rubber gloves. Remember the golden rule: the smaller the chile, the hotter it is.

Dried chiles

Ancho: these are dried poblano chiles. Relatively mild, they are a wrinkled deep, reddish-brown color.

Chipotle: these brick-red dried jalapeño chiles can be bought dried or canned.

Mulato: these pungent brownish-red chiles are mild to moderate in their heat and intensity.

Note: all dried chiles should be soaked in warm water for at least 30 minutes before using.

Chocolate (cocoa)

Legend has it that Quetzacoatl, the Aztec god of light, taught the Mexicans how to grow cocoa and make chocolate, the sacred drink of the gods. The Aztecs roasted and ground the cocoa beans, and then mixed them with water to make a hot chocolate drink, sweetened with honey and flavored with vanilla and spices. Only the elite ruling class drank

chocolate, and it is still prepared in the traditional way, by whisking with a carved wooden *molinillo* until it is frothy. Chocolate is also used in some savory dishes, and it is always added to *mole*, Mexico's most famous dish.

Cilantro

This herb is not indigenous to Mexico; it was probably introduced by the Spanish after the conquest. It has become the most favored herb of Mexican cooks and is used in most savory dishes. It resembles flat-leaf parsley but has a very distinctive intense flavor and there is no real substitute. Oregano and parsley are also used to flavor dishes as is epazote.

Salsas

These are sauces which are usually made from chiles and tomatoes and are served with cooked fish, meat, poultry, beans and eggs, or added to tortillas before stuffing. In the West and in Tex-Mex cooking, which is widespread in the United States, hot, fiery salsas are used as dips for *totopos* (fried tortilla chips).

Seviche

This method of "cooking" raw fish or seafood by marinating it in lime or lemon juice is common in Mexico and throughout Latin America. The fish should be marinated for about three to five hours until it loses its translucence and looks "cooked." It is usually eaten as a first course before the main course.

Shortening

This is commonly used for frying beans and other foods. Fat back bacon is also popular but oils are seldom favored. However, you can substitute olive, vegetable or sunflower oils instead.

Tequila

This is the fiery spirit of Mexico, made from the fermented sap of the maguey plant. It is the basis of Margaritas, which are now drunk all over the world. In Mexico, tequila is usually served neat in small glasses, frosted with salt around the rim, embellished only with a slice of fresh lime.

Tomatoes

The Mexicans use red or green (husk) tomatoes. They are used in fresh and cooked sauces and in making guacamole. The little green tomatoes, *tomatillos*, are very popular with a delicate flavor. They are not the same as unripe green tomatoes, but have a loose outer covering. They are available canned outside of Mexico, and may be grown from seed.

Tortillas

These are unique to Mexico and were traditionally made from ground corn husks. Now they are made from *masa harina*, a fine dried corn flour, or from wheat flour. What makes them unusual is that, unlike other breads, they are made from cooked flour as the dried corn has already been boiled, dried and ground to make the instant masa.

The cooked tortillas are stacked up in a basket and wrapped in a cloth to keep them warm before serving with every meal. They are used in a variety of Mexican dishes:

Burritos: stuffed tortilla parcels.
Enchiladas: tortillas dipped in chile sauce, filled and baked.
Flautas: tortillas rolled tightly into cylinders around a filling and fried.
Quesadillas: tortillas folded over cheese and then fried.
Tacos: tortillas stuffed and rolled into cylinders, eaten soft or fried.
Tostadas: crisp, fried tortillas topped with meat or beans and served with salsa and guacamole.
Totopos: tortillas cut into wedges and fried until crisp and golden. They are sprinkled with coarsely ground salt and may be used as dippers for guacamole or refried beans.

Cooking equipment

In the traditional Mexican kitchen, there are only a few basic cooking utensils.

Cazuelas: together with *ollas*, these are the earthenware casseroles and claypots used for cooking stews and *moles*. Rough on the outside, they are glazed and smooth on the inside. Before using for the first time, they must be seasoned. Mexican cooks do this by rubbing them with a clove of garlic and then filling with cold water and a bundle of fresh herbs. The pots are then baked in a moderate oven or simmered on top of the stove for several hours until the water evaporates, leaving the pot dry.

Comal: this is a griddle used for cooking tortillas.

Metate: this is a heavy three-legged stone, made of basalt and used for grinding corn, cocoa and chiles.

Molcajete and tejolote: this heavy mortar and pestle consists of a round volcanic bowl on three legs and a pestle made of black basalt. It is used for grinding chiles and spices.

Tortilla press: although tortillas are traditionally made by hand, patting and slapping them into shape, it is easier to use a cast-iron or steel tortilla press to flatten the dough to a small thin round.

TORTILLAS

Flour tortillas

3 cups all-purpose flour
2 teaspoons baking soda
3/4 teaspoon salt
2 tablespoons shortening
1 cup warm water

1 Sift the flour, baking soda and salt into a bowl. Cut the shortening into tiny pieces and add to the flour. Gradually stir in enough warm water to form a soft dough.

3 Roll a ball of dough out into a round, about 7 inches in diameter, on a lightly floured surface. Repeat this process with the other balls of dough.

4 Heat an ungreased griddle or cast-iron skillet until it is very hot. Put a tortilla on the griddle and cook over moderately high heat until bubbles start to appear. Turn the tortilla over and cook the other side, gently pressing out the bubbles that form, until golden brown. The cooked tortillas should be soft and pliable. Stack them up and keep them warm while you cook the remaining tortillas.

2 Turn the dough out on to a lightly floured surface and knead until smooth and elastic. Divide into 12 small portions and shape each into a ball. Cover with a cloth and leave to rest for 15-20 minutes.

PREPARATION: 30-35 MINUTES
COOKING: 10 MINUTES
SERVES: 6-8

GUACAMOLE

Avocado dip with tortilla chips

2 large ripe avocados

3 tablespoons lemon or lime juice

2 garlic cloves, minced

$^1/_3$ cup chopped scallions

1-2 tablespoons chopped mild green chiles or jalapeños

2 tablespoons chopped fresh cilantro

salt and black pepper

$^1/_2$ cup skinned, seeded and chopped tomatoes

For the totopos:

8 corn or wheat tortillas

oil for deep-frying

sea salt

2 Put the avocado flesh in a mixing bowl with the remaining lemon or lime juice, and mash coarsely. Add the garlic, scallions, chiles and cilantro and some seasoning to taste. Mix in the chopped tomatoes. Cover the bowl and place in the refrigerator for at least 1 hour.

1 Cut the avocados in half, and carefully remove the peel and pits. Scoop out the flesh and sprinkle with a little of the lemon or lime juice to prevent it from discoloring.

PREPARATION: 15 MINUTES +
1 HOUR CHILLING
COOKING: 5 MINUTES
SERVES: 6

3 Meanwhile, make the totopos (tortilla chips) to serve with the guacamole. Cut each tortilla into 8 equal-sized pieces.

4 Deep-fry the tortillas in hot oil until they are crisp and golden. Drain on paper towels and sprinkle with a little sea salt. Serve with the guacamole.

NACHOS

Spicy tortilla chips with cheese

1 Make the chile sauce: heat the oil in a small saucepan and sauté the onion and garlic until soft and golden, stirring occasionally.

2 Add the tomatoes, chiles, oregano, cumin and seasoning. Bring to the boil and then reduce the heat and simmer gently for 15 minutes, or until the chile sauce is thickened and reduced.

3 Arrange the tortilla chips on a large ovenproof dish or plate and then carefully spoon the chile sauce over the top of them.

4 Sprinkle with grated cheese and cook in a preheated oven at 350° until the cheese melts and starts to bubble. Serve the nachos with the sour cream and guacamole, garnished with diced onion and tomato.

2 tablespoons oil
1 onion, chopped
2 garlic cloves, minced
4 large tomatoes, skinned and chopped
1 cup canned jalapeño chiles or 2 fresh red chiles, seeded and chopped
pinch of dried oregano
pinch of ground cumin
salt and pepper
½ pound tortilla chips (see page 12)
1 cup grated cheese
½ cup sour cream
1 cup guacamole
To garnish:
diced onion and tomato

PREPARATION: 30 MINUTES
COOKING: 10 MINUTES
SERVES: 4-6

QUESADILLAS
Cheese-stuffed tortillas

1 Put the tortillas on a board and divide the refried bean mixture between them, putting a spoonful of mixture on half of each tortilla and leaving a little space around the edge of the loaded side.

2 Put a little grated cheese and some sliced Mozzarella on top of the refried beans, and then a few slices of chile. Fold the tortilla over the top of the filling.

3 Press the edges of each folded tortilla firmly together between your fingertips. It helps if the tortillas are soft and quite damp when you do this. If necessary, secure them with wooden toothpicks. Cover the folded tortillas with a damp cloth while you make the remaining quesadillas.

4 Heat some oil in a large pan to a depth of 1½ inches, and fry the quesadillas, a few at a time, until crisp and golden brown. Remove and drain on paper towels. Serve the quesadillas hot with salsa, guacamole and sour cream.

PREPARATION: 15 MINUTES
COOKING: 5-10 MINUTES
SERVES: 4-6

12 soft flour or corn tortillas
6 ounces refried beans (see page 82)
2 cups Monterey Jack cheese, grated
1¼ cups Mozzarella cheese, cut into strips
4-6 fresh green chiles, seeded and thinly sliced
oil for cooking
To serve:
salsa, guacamole, sour cream

FLAUTAS

Tortilla flutes

14 ounces refried beans (see page 82)

2 fresh green chiles, chopped

¼ cup chopped onion

¼ cup toasted chopped almonds

2 tablespoons chopped fresh cilantro

1 cup grated cheese

8 corn or flour tortillas

oil for frying

To serve:

red chile sauce (see page 110)

1 avocado, pitted, peeled and sliced

2 Meanwhile, wrap the tortillas in foil and warm in a low oven to soften them. Spoon a little of the refried bean and cheese mixture along the center of each warmed tortilla.

1 Put the refried beans and chiles in a pan and heat through gently, stirring occasionally so that they do not stick. Mix in the onion, almonds, cilantro and cheese.

3 Roll up each tortilla carefully and tightly to form a flute. If necessary, secure with wooden toothpicks to prevent them from opening during the frying process.

4 Heat the oil, about 1 inch deep, in a heavy skillet and fry the flautas in batches until they are crisp and lightly browned all over. Drain on some paper towels. Serve the flautas with red chile sauce and sliced avocado.

PREPARATION: 20 MINUTES
COOKING: 10 MINUTES
SERVES: 4

HUEVOS RANCHEROS

Baked ranch-style eggs

2 onions, finely chopped
3 garlic cloves, minced
2 sweet red peppers, seeded and chopped
2 fresh red chiles, seeded and chopped
2 tablespoons shortening
1 teaspoon dried oregano
$1/2$ teaspoon ground cumin
salt and pepper
4 large tomatoes, skinned and chopped
$1/2$ cup tomato paste
$1/2$ cup water or stock
4 eggs
1 tablespoon chopped fresh cilantro
1 large avocado, pitted, peeled and sliced

2 Add the chopped tomatoes and the tomato paste together with $1/2$ cup water (or stock if wished). Bring to the boil and then reduce the heat and simmer gently until the sauce reduces and thickens.

3 Pour the prepared tomato sauce into a large greased ovenproof dish and then make 4 wells, or indentations, in the tomato sauce with the back of a spoon.

1 Sauté the onions, garlic, sweet peppers and chiles in the shortening until soft and golden. Add the oregano, cumin and seasoning to taste. Stir into the onion and pepper mixture and cook for 2 minutes.

4 Carefully break an egg into each well. Bake in a preheated oven at 350° for about 10-12 minutes, until the eggs are set and cooked. Serve sprinkled with chopped cilantro and garnished with avocado slices.

PREPARATION: 25 MINUTES
COOKING: 10-12 MINUTES
SERVES: 4

AGUACATES RELLENOS
Stuffed avocados

2 tablespoons olive oil
1 teaspoon wine vinegar
juice of ½ lime
salt and freshly ground black pepper
2 avocados
For the stuffing:
3 tablespoons olive oil
1 onion, finely chopped
1 garlic clove, minced
1¼ cups chopped mushrooms
1 red chile, finely chopped
1 tablespoon chopped fresh cilantro
To serve:
sour cream
warm tortillas

2 Cut the avocados in half and remove the pits. Brush the inner surfaces of the avocado halves with the lime dressing; this will add flavor and prevent them from browning. Set aside while you prepare the stuffing.

3 Heat the olive oil in a heavy skillet and sauté the onion and garlic over low heat until soft and golden. Add the chopped mushrooms and chile, and continue cooking for a few minutes, stirring occasionally, until cooked and golden brown. Stir in the cilantro.

1 Make the dressing for the stuffed avocados: blend the olive oil with the wine vinegar and lime juice in a small bowl until thoroughly combined. Season with a little salt and some freshly ground black pepper.

4 Remove from the heat and pile the stuffing mixture into the prepared avocados. Place on a lightly oiled baking tray and warm through in a preheated oven at 325° for 10-15 minutes. Serve topped with sour cream, with warm tortillas.

PREPARATION: 25 MINUTES
COOKING: 10-15 MINUTES
SERVES: 4

GAZPACHO

Iced tomato soup

1 garlic clove

4 cups tomato juice

3 tablespoons olive oil

2 tablespoons lemon juice

1 tablespoon lime juice

2 teaspoons sugar

salt and black pepper

1/2 cup diced peeled cucumber

1/2 cup chopped mild red onion or scallions

1/2 cup diced sweet red pepper

1/4 cup diced avocado

2 tablespoons chopped mixed fresh herbs

For serving:

ice cubes

coarsely crushed tortilla chips

lime wedges

2 Pour the tomato juice into the bowl, and then add the olive oil, lemon and lime juices, sugar and salt and black pepper to taste.

3 Lightly beat the tomato juice with the other ingredients until well amalgamated. Cover the bowl with some plastic wrap and chill in the refrigerator for at least 1 hour.

4 Beat the soup again and stir in the remaining ingredients. Place some ice cubes in individual serving bowls and pour the soup over the top. Sprinkle with coarsely crushed tortilla chips and serve with lime wedges.

1 Cut the garlic clove in half and then rub the cut surfaces over the bottom and around the sides of a large mixing bowl. Discard the garlic.

PREPARATION: 20 MINUTES
CHILLING: 1 HOUR
SERVES: 6-8

SOPA DE AGUACATE FRIA

Cold avocado soup

¼ cup butter
4 tablespoons olive oil
1 onion, finely chopped
1 leek, finely chopped
1 carrot, finely chopped
2 garlic cloves, minced
4 ripe avocados, peeled and pitted
1 cup natural yogurt
salt and ground black pepper
2 tablespoons lime juice
½ cup crème fraîche
2 tablespoons chopped fresh cilantro

For the stock:

8 cups water
bones from 1 chicken
1 onion, sliced
4 garlic cloves, halved
2 carrots
2 bay leaves
few black peppercorns
½ teaspoon salt
2 sticks celery

2 Melt the butter and oil in a large saucepan and sauté the onion, leek, carrot and garlic until tender. Add about 3 cups of the reserved chicken stock and simmer gently for about 30 minutes.

3 Process the avocados in batches with 4 cups of the reserved stock in a food processor or blender until smooth. Add the vegetable mixture and continue to blend to a smooth green purée.

4 Stir in the yogurt and season to taste with salt and pepper. Add the lime juice, and thin with stock if necessary. Chill for 1 hour. Serve with a swirl of crème fraîche, sprinkled with chopped cilantro.

1 Make the stock: bring the water to the boil in a large saucepan or stock pot and add the chicken bones, vegetables, herbs and seasoning. Skim off any scum, lower the heat and simmer for 1½ hours. Cool and strain.

PREPARATION: 15 MINUTES
COOKING: 2 HOURS +
CHILLING TIME
SERVES: 6-8

26

SOPA DE FRIJOLES NEGROS

Black bean soup

1 Place the black beans in a bowl and cover with cold water. Leave them to soak overnight. The following day, drain the beans and rinse them well.

2 Put the beans in a large saucepan, cover with fresh, cold water and bring to the boil. Boil briskly for 10 minutes, drain and rinse well. Return the beans to the pan with the ham, onion, celery, garlic and measured water. Bring to the boil, skimming off any scum. Add the spices and herbs, cover and simmer for 3-4 hours.

PREPARATION: 6-8 HOURS
COOKING: 5¼ HOURS
SERVES: 4-6

3 Remove the ham (use in another dish) and discard the bay leaf. Let the bean mixture cool and then process in batches in a food processor or blender, reserving a few whole beans for decoration.

1 pound dried black beans
1-1½ pounds smoked ham hocks
1 large onion, quartered
1 celery stick, chopped
3 garlic cloves, peeled
8 cups water
1 teaspoon black peppercorns
4 whole cloves
½ teaspoon cumin seeds
1 bay leaf
2 teaspoons minced garlic
salt
1 cup dry sherry
To garnish:
lemon slices

4 Sieve the puréed mixture into a clean saucepan and add the minced garlic, and season to taste with salt. Simmer for 45 minutes and then stir in the sherry. Simmer for 20 minutes, until thick. Stir in the reserved beans and serve hot, garnished with lemon slices.

29

ALBONDIGAS DE CAMARONES

Mexican shrimp soup

½ pound cooked shrimp, shelled and finely chopped

2 tablespoons minced onion

1 tablespoon tomato paste

1 teaspoon ground cinnamon

1 teaspoon ground cumin

1 teaspoon chopped oregano

1 teaspoon ground coriander seeds

2 heaped tablespoons all-purpose flour

1 egg yolk

pinch of salt

For the soup:

3 tablespoons olive oil

1 onion, thinly sliced

2 cloves garlic, minced

1 pound tomatoes, skinned and chopped

4 green chiles, seeded and chopped

1½ quarts fish stock

2 bay leaves

salt and freshly ground black pepper

2 tablespoons chopped fresh cilantro

2 Make the soup: heat the olive oil in a large saucepan and sauté the sliced onion and garlic for 10 minutes, until soft. Add the chopped tomatoes and chiles and cook over low heat for 15 minutes.

3 Add the fish stock, bay leaves, salt and pepper, and then bring to the boil. Simmer the soup very gently for 30 minutes over low heat.

4 Divide the shrimp mixture into 12 portions and shape into small balls. Drop them carefully into the soup. Poach very gently over low heat for 5 minutes. Remove the bay leaves and serve hot, sprinkled with chopped cilantro.

1 Put the chopped shrimp in a bowl with the onion, tomato paste, spices, herbs, flour, egg yolk and salt. Mix well until thoroughly blended, then cover the bowl and chill in the refrigerator for 30 minutes.

PREPARATION: 20 MINUTES
COOKING: 1 HOUR
SERVES: 4-6

SOPA DE TORTILLA

Tortilla soup

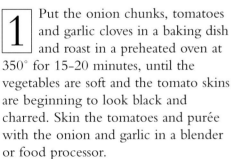

1 Put the onion chunks, tomatoes and garlic cloves in a baking dish and roast in a preheated oven at 350° for 15-20 minutes, until the vegetables are soft and the tomato skins are beginning to look black and charred. Skin the tomatoes and purée with the onion and garlic in a blender or food processor.

1 large onion, cut in chunks
3 large tomatoes
3 garlic cloves, peeled
4 tablespoons olive oil
4½ cups chicken stock
salt and freshly ground black pepper
6 x 1-day-old tortillas
oil for shallow-frying
2 fresh red or green chiles, seeded and chopped

To serve:

chopped avocado
sour cream
lime wedges

2 Heat 2 tablespoons of the oil and sauté the puréed mixture for a few minutes. Simmer until it is thick and reduced. Add the chicken stock and bring to the boil. Reduce the heat, season with salt and pepper and simmer, covered, for 15-20 minutes.

3 Cut the tortillas into thin strips and shallow-fry in some oil until golden brown. Drain on some paper towels and then add to the soup. Simmer the tortilla soup gently for a further 5 minutes.

4 Fry the chiles in the remaining olive oil in a small skillet until crisp. Serve the soup garnished with the fried chiles, some chopped avocado, sour cream and lime wedges.

PREPARATION: 20-25 MINUTES
COOKING: 35-40 MINUTES
SERVES: 4-6

SEVICHE

Marinated fish

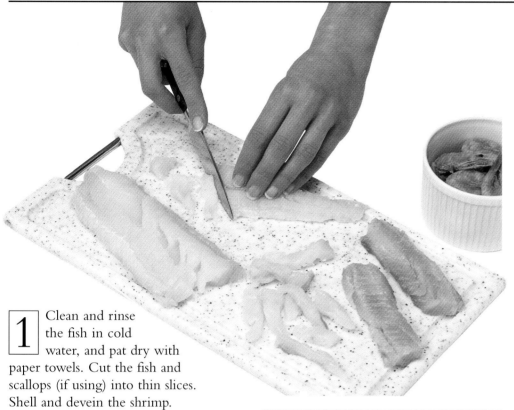

1 pound mixed fish, e.g fillets of sole, flounder, haddock, shucked scallops and shrimp
1/2 cup lime juice
1/2 teaspoon dried red chile flakes
2 tomatoes
1 tablespoon olive oil
1/2 teaspoon salt
pinch of dried oregano
freshly ground black pepper
For the garnish:
peeled, sliced avocado
2 tablespoons chopped fresh cilantro
2 limes, cut into wedges

1 Clean and rinse the fish in cold water, and pat dry with paper towels. Cut the fish and scallops (if using) into thin slices. Shell and devein the shrimp.

2 Place all the fish in a ceramic bowl and pour the lime juice over the top. Cover and then refrigerate for about 3-4 hours.

3 Put the tomatoes in a bowl and cover with boiling water. Leave for 1 minute and then plunge them into a bowl of cold water and skin them. Chop them roughly.

4 Stir in the dried chile flakes, tomato, olive oil, salt, oregano and pepper. Mix well and refrigerate for 2-3 hours. Stand at room temperature for 15 minutes before serving, garnished with avocado, chopped cilantro and lime wedges.

PREPARATION: 15 MINUTES
MARINATING: 3-4 HOURS
SERVES: 4

HUACHINANGO EN CILANTRO

Red snapper in cilantro

2 pounds red snapper or other white fish fillets

4 tablespoons lime or lemon juice

2 teaspoons salt

4 tablespoons olive oil

½ cup fresh breadcrumbs

1 garlic clove, minced

6 tablespoons crushed cilantro leaves

1 teaspoon grated lime or lemon peel

freshly ground black pepper

For serving:

warmed tortillas

1 Rinse the fish fillets under running cold water and pat dry with paper towels. Rub the fish with half of the lime or lemon juice and 1 teaspoon of the salt, and place, skin-side down, in a lightly oiled heavy skillet.

2 Add sufficient cold water to cover the fish and then simmer gently over low heat for 5 minutes, turning twice during the cooking time.

3 In another skillet, heat half of the olive oil, and add the breadcrumbs, garlic, remaining salt and 4 tablespoons of the cilantro. Cook over a low heat, stirring constantly, until the crumbs are golden brown. Spread over the fish and simmer for 7-10 minutes, until the fish flakes easily.

4 Blend the remaining lime or lemon juice and oil together, and pour over the fish. Cook for 2-3 minutes. Combine the remaining cilantro with the grated lime or lemon peel and sprinkle over the fish. Season with black pepper and serve hot with warmed tortillas.

PREPARATION: 10 MINUTES
COOKING: 20 MINUTES
SERVES: 4

PESCADO VERACRUZ

Veracruz-style fish

4 tablespoons olive oil
2 onions, chopped
1 garlic clove, minced
2 fresh hot red chiles, seeded and finely chopped
4 large tomatoes, skinned and chopped
8 stuffed green olives, chopped
4 pitted ripe olives, chopped
1 tablespoon chopped capers
pinch of dried oregano
2 pounds sea bass or red snapper fillets
$1/3$ cup all-purpose flour
salt
$1/4$ cup butter
2 tablespoons chopped fresh cilantro

1 Heat the oil in a skillet, add the onion and garlic and fry gently until soft and golden. Stir in the chiles, chopped tomatoes, olives, capers and oregano. Bring to the boil, reduce the heat and simmer the mixture gently for 20 minutes.

3 Melt the butter in a large skillet, add the fish fillets and fry gently for about 5 minutes on each side until cooked and golden.

2 Wash the sea bass or red snapper fillets and pat dry on paper towels. Mix the flour with a little salt to season it in a dish, and then use to lightly coat the fish fillets, shaking off any excess flour.

4 Transfer the fish fillets to a heated serving dish and pour the tomato sauce over the top. Sprinkle with chopped cilantro and serve with warm tortillas, salad and rice.

PREPARATION: 15 MINUTES
COOKING: 35 MINUTES
SERVES: 4–6

PESCADO MEXICANO

Mexican fish stew

3 tablespoons olive oil

1 large onion, chopped

2 garlic cloves, minced

1 sweet red pepper, seeded and chopped

1 sweet yellow pepper, seeded and chopped

1 pound tomatoes, skinned and chopped

2 tablespoons finely chopped fresh ginger

1 tablespoon chopped fresh cilantro

2 teaspoons chopped fresh oregano

grated peel of 1 lime

few drops of hot chile sauce

2-4 dried red chiles, chopped

2½ pounds angler fish

1¼ cups fish stock or clam juice

12 scallops, halved

½ pound uncooked shrimp

salt and freshly ground black pepper

torn cilantro leaves

2 Add the tomato, ginger, chopped cilantro, oregano, lime peel, chile sauce and dried red chiles. Stir well to mix thoroughly and then simmer the mixture gently over low heat for 10 minutes.

3 Cut the angler fish into chunks, removing any bone and skin. Add the angler fish and fish stock to the saucepan and bring to the boil. Reduce the heat and then simmer gently for 20 minutes.

1 Heat the oil in a large heavy-based saucepan and gently sauté the onion, garlic and the red and yellow peppers for about 10-15 minutes, until they are tender.

4 Stir in the scallops and shrimp and cook gently for 2 more minutes, until cooked. Season to taste with salt and pepper and serve the fish stew with warm tortillas garnished with torn cilantro leaves.

PREPARATION: 15 MINUTES
COOKING: 45 MINUTES
SERVES: 6

ENCHILADAS DE JAIBA

Crab-stuffed tortillas

oil for shallow-frying

12 soft corn tortillas

1¹/₂ cups red chile sauce (see page 110)

1 pound crabmeat

2 cups grated Monterey Jack cheese

1¹/₄ cups diced Mozzarella cheese

1 small red onion, finely chopped

3 tablespoons chopped fresh cilantro

For the garnish:

sour cream and guacamole

1 Heat the oil in a large skillet and shallow-fry the tortillas, one at a time, over moderate heat for a few seconds until they become limp. Take care not to overcook the tortillas – they must not be allowed to become crisp.

3 Put some crabmeat on the middle of each tortilla. Sprinkle some grated cheese with the diced Mozzarella on top (reserving a little) and then add some chopped red onion. Roll up the tortillas and place them in a well-buttered ovenproof dish.

2 Pat the tortillas with paper towels to remove excess oil and then spread each one with a little of the prepared red chile sauce.

4 Pour the remaining red chile sauce over the top of the tortillas and scatter with the rest of the cheese. Bake in a preheated oven at 400° for 15-20 minutes. Garnish with chopped cilantro and serve the enchiladas with sour cream and guacamole.

PREPARATION: 15 MINUTES
COOKING: 15-20 MINUTES
SERVES: 4-6

EMPANADAS DE CAMARONES
Shrimp turnovers

1 Heat the oil in a skillet, add the onion and garlic and sauté over low heat until soft and golden. Stir in the tomato paste, shrimp, chiles, cumin, allspice, oregano, lemon juice and seasoning. Cook gently until the mixture reduces and thickens a little, then set aside to cool.

| 2 tablespoons olive oil |
| 1 large onion, finely chopped |
| 2 garlic cloves, minced |
| 4 tablespoons tomato paste |
| 1 pound cooked shrimp, chopped |
| 4 green chiles, seeded and finely chopped |
| 1 teaspoon ground cumin |
| 1 teaspoon ground allspice |
| 2 teaspoons oregano |
| 1 tablespoon lemon juice |
| salt and freshly ground pepper to taste |
| tortilla dough (see page 10) |
| oil for deep-frying |

To serve:

salsa and guacamole

2 Roll out the tortilla dough and make about 20 tortillas, 3 inches in diameter. Place a small spoonful of the cooled shrimp mixture in the center of each tortilla.

PREPARATION: 25 MINUTES
COOKING: 20-25 MINUTES
SERVES: 5-6

3 Fold the dough over the shrimp filling and dampen and press the edges together firmly between your fingers to seal them. Repeat in this way until all the empanadas are sealed. If wished, cover with plastic wrap and chill in the refrigerator until you are ready to cook and serve them.

4 Heat the oil in a large saucepan and deep-fry the empanadas until they are golden all over. Drain on paper towels and serve hot with salsa and guacamole.

CAMARONES ACAPULQUENOS
Acapulco-style shrimp

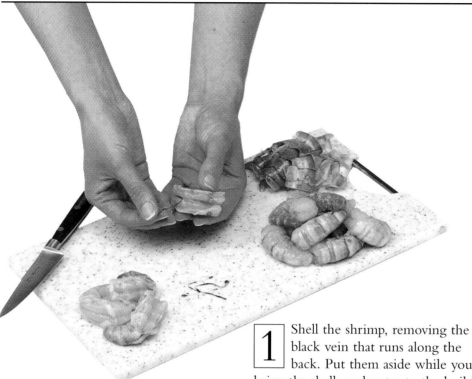

1 Shell the shrimp, removing the black vein that runs along the back. Put them aside while you bring the shells and water to the boil in a small pan. Simmer gently for 15-20 minutes, and then strain into a clean jug, discarding the shells.

3 Add the tomatoes, tomato paste and lime juice. Season to taste with salt and freshly ground black pepper, and simmer for 10-15 minutes until the mixture thickens and reduces.

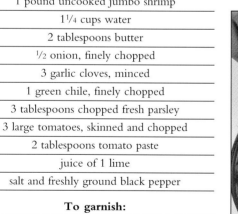

1 pound uncooked jumbo shrimp
1¼ cups water
2 tablespoons butter
½ onion, finely chopped
3 garlic cloves, minced
1 green chile, finely chopped
3 tablespoons chopped fresh parsley
3 large tomatoes, skinned and chopped
2 tablespoons tomato paste
juice of 1 lime
salt and freshly ground black pepper

To garnish:

2 tablespoons chopped fresh parsley
wedges of lime
boiled rice

PREPARATION: 30 MINUTES
COOKING: 20-25 MINUTES
SERVES: 4

2 Heat the butter in a large heavy-based skillet and sauté the onion and garlic until soft and golden. Add the chile and parsley, and sauté, stirring, for about 2 minutes, until the parsley turns dark green.

4 Add the reserved shrimp liquid and simmer for 5 minutes, stirring occasionally. Gently stir in the peeled shrimp and cook for a further 2-3 minutes until they turn pink. Serve garnished with chopped parsley and lime wedges on a bed of rice.

CAMARONES AL CARBON
Seafood brochettes

1 Prepare the seafood: peel the shrimp and remove the black vein running along the back. Remove any bones from the tuna and cut into large chunks. Shuck and wash the scallops and pat them dry. If they are very large, cut them in half.

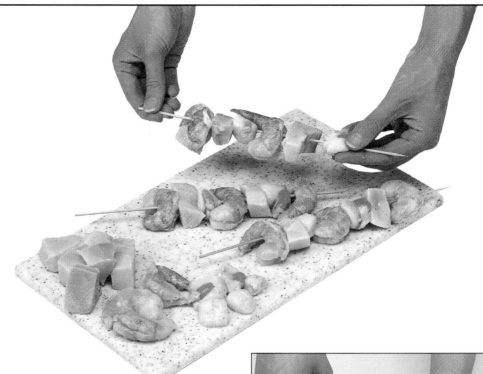

2 Make the marinade: put the squeezed juice of 2 limes with the olive oil and garlic in a large bowl. Mix thoroughly to blend and add some salt and pepper. Put the prepared seafood in the marinade and stir gently until it is completely coated. Cover and chill for at least 1 hour.

3 Remove the seafood from the marinade and thread alternately on to wooden or metal skewers. Place them on the rack of a broiler pan and brush with the remaining marinade. Broil, turning occasionally, until cooked and tender – this takes about 5 minutes. Baste with more marinade if necessary.

4 Make the chile butter: blend the softened butter with the chopped chiles until they are thoroughly mixed. Arrange the seafood brochettes on 4 serving plates on a bed of rice and put a pat of chile butter on top of each one. Scatter with torn cilantro leaves.

1 pound mixed seafood (e.g. uncooked shrimp, fresh tuna, scallops)
juice of 2 limes
2 tablespoons olive oil
2 garlic cloves, minced
salt and freshly ground black pepper
¼ cup softened butter
2 hot chiles (preferably jalapeño)
few cilantro leaves, torn
To serve:
plain boiled rice

PREPARATION: 20 MINUTES +
1 HOUR MARINATING
COOKING: 5 MINUTES
SERVES: 4

CAMARONES AL MOJO DE AJO
Garlic shrimp

Coat the prepared shrimp with this garlic mixture and place them in a bowl. Scrape out any of the remaining garlic paste over the top, then cover the bowl and refrigerate for at least 1 hour.

1 Prepare the shrimp: remove the heads and, leaving them in their shells, split them carefully down the middle towards the tail end without completely separating them. They should look a little like butterflies. Remove the dark vein running along the back of the shrimp.

24 uncooked jumbo shrimp	
6 garlic cloves	
sea salt and whole black peppercorns	
2 red chiles, seeded and chopped	
3 tablespoons olive oil	
¼ cup butter	
juice of 2 limes	
3 tablespoons chopped fresh cilantro	
To serve:	
lime wedges	
sliced avocado	
warm tortillas	

PREPARATION: 15 MINUTES +
1 HOUR MARINATING
COOKING: 5 MINUTES
SERVES: 4-6

2 Peel the garlic cloves and then mince them with the sea salt, peppercorns and the chopped chiles in a pestle and mortar, until you have a thick aromatic paste.

4 Heat the olive oil and butter in a large heavy-based skillet and add the shrimp and the garlic paste. Quickly sauté them over medium heat for 2-3 minutes, until they turn pink. Remove and keep warm. Add the lime juice to the skillet and stir into the juices. Boil vigorously for a couple of minutes and then pour over the shrimp. Serve sprinkled with cilantro, with lime wedges, sliced avocado and freshly-made warm tortillas.

MOLE DE POLLO

Chicken stew

1 chicken, cut into 4 pieces
1 garlic clove, minced
1 onion, chopped
1 dried red chile, seeded and chopped
2 cups water or chicken stock
1 fresh green or red chile, chopped
³/₄ cup flaked almonds
1¹/₂ cups fresh breadcrumbs
¹/₂ teaspoon ground cinnamon
¹/₂ teaspoon ground cloves
1 tablespoon sesame seeds
2 tablespoons shortening
1³/₄ cups canned tomatoes, drained and chopped
1 square unsweetened dark chocolate, grated
salt and pepper
2 tablespoons sesame seeds, toasted
2 limes, cut into wedges
a few fresh cilantro leaves

2 In a blender or food processor, blend together the chile, almonds, breadcrumbs, cinnamon, cloves and sesame seeds. Add about half of the reserved chicken stock and blend until smooth.

4 Add the chicken pieces and bring to the boil. Cook gently to heat the chicken through, and then transfer to a serving dish. Serve sprinkled with toasted sesame seeds, and garnished with lime wedges and cilantro leaves.

3 Heat the shortening in a skillet and stir in the breadcrumb mixture. Fry gently for 2 minutes and then add the tomatoes. Gradually stir in the remaining stock, together with the grated chocolate. Simmer gently for 5 minutes and season to taste.

1 Simmer the chicken pieces with the garlic, onion and dried chile in the water or chicken stock for 40 minutes, or until the chicken is tender. Cool slightly, strain the stock and skim off any fat. Measure out 2 cups and set aside. Remove the skin and bones from the chicken and cut into neat pieces.

PREPARATION: 20 MINUTES
COOKING: 1 HOUR
SERVES: 4

FAJITAS DE POLLO
Chicken-stuffed tortillas

6 chicken breast fillets, skinned and boned and cut into pieces

2 large onions, peeled and sliced

1 sweet red pepper, seeded and cut into strips

1 sweet green pepper, seeded and cut into strips

2 tablespoons olive oil

12 soft tortillas, warmed

1/2 pound guacamole

1 1/4 cups sour cream

2 tablespoons toasted sesame seeds

1 tablespoon chopped fresh cilantro

For the marinade:

juice of 4 limes

3 tablespoons olive oil

1 teaspoon dried oregano

1 teaspoon dried cilantro

1 Make the marinade: combine the lime juice with the oil, dried oregano and cilantro in a bowl. Add the chicken and stir well. Cover and leave in the refrigerator for 4 hours.

PREPARATION: 15 MINUTES
MARINATING: 4 HOURS
COOKING: 45 MINUTES
SERVES: 4

2 Put the chicken and the marinade in a roasting pan. Cover with foil and bake in a preheated oven at 400° for 30 minutes. Bake uncovered for the last 10 minutes of the cooking time. Slice the chicken into thin strips.

3 Meanwhile, sauté the onions and sweet peppers in the oil until they are soft and melting. It does not matter if they become a little brown and caramelized.

4 Place a little of the sautéed onions and sweet peppers on each warmed tortilla and top with some chicken. Add a little guacamole, some sour cream and sesame seeds. Sprinkle with cilantro and roll up. Serve with salsa if wished.

POLLO CON NARANJAS

Orange chicken

1 teaspoon salt

$^1/_4$ teaspoon ground cinnamon

$^1/_8$ teaspoon ground cloves

1 chicken, cut into 4 pieces

2 tablespoons oil

1 onion, chopped

2 garlic cloves, minced

$^2/_3$ cup fresh orange juice

$^2/_3$ cup chicken stock

2 tablespoons raisins

2 green chiles, seeded and sliced

$^1/_2$ cup slivered almonds

3 oranges, peeled and thinly sliced

2 tablespoons chopped fresh cilantro

2 Heat the oil in a large skillet, add the chicken and fry, turning occasionally, until all the chicken pieces are browned all over. Remove them from the skillet and pour off any excess fat. Keep the chicken warm.

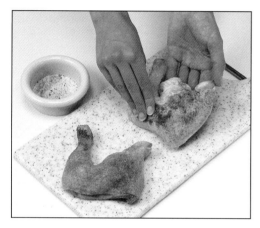

1 Mix the salt, ground cinnamon and cloves together, and then rub this spicy mixture all over the chicken pieces to flavor them.

3 Add the onion and garlic and fry gently until tender and golden. Return the chicken to the skillet and stir in the orange juice, chicken stock, raisins and chiles. Cover and simmer for 1 hour, or until the chicken is cooked and tender.

4 Add the almonds and the orange slices, and stir gently. Heat through over low heat for about 5 minutes. Serve the orange chicken sprinkled with chopped cilantro.

PREPARATION: 15 MINUTES
COOKING: 1½ HOURS
SERVES: 4

POLLO AL CARBON

Marinated chicken kebabs

juice of 2 limes or lemons

1 tablespoon honey

1 green chile, finely chopped

2 tablespoons olive oil

6 chicken breasts

For the avocado sauce:

3 tablespoons olive oil

1 tablespoon red wine vinegar

1 large avocado, peeled, stoned and puréed

1 large tomato, skinned and chopped

2 scallions, chopped

$^{1}/_{2}$ cup sour cream

seeds of 1 pomegranate

2 Bone and skin the chicken breasts and cut the flesh into large chunks. Add to the marinade and stir gently until thoroughly coated. Cover and chill for at least 1 hour.

1 Make the marinade: squeeze the lime or lemon juice into a large bowl and mix in the honey, chopped chile and olive oil, until the mixture is well blended and smooth.

PREPARATION: 15 MINUTES +
1 HOUR MARINATING
COOKING: 15 MINUTES
SERVES: 4

3 Thread the chicken on to wooden skewers and brush with the marinade. Place under a preheated hot broiler or cook on a barbecue, turning occasionally, until the chicken is cooked, tender and golden brown. Brush the kebabs with more marinade if necessary.

4 Meanwhile, make the avocado sauce: blend the olive oil and vinegar together in a bowl and then beat in the puréed avocado until thick and smooth. Stir in the chopped tomato and scallions, and then the sour cream. Serve the kebabs accompanied by a mound of avocado sauce, scattered with pomegranate seeds.

POSOLE

Pork and chicken stew

1 Put the cubed pork, ribs and onion in a large saucepan and pour in 2 quarts of the water. Bring to the boil, skimming off any scum. Add the garlic, lower the heat and then simmer for 1 hour. Add the chicken and the remaining water and simmer for 30 minutes.

³/₄ pound boneless pork shoulder, cubed
¹/₂ pound pork ribs
1 large onion, quartered
3 quarts water
2 garlic cloves, minced
2¹/₂ pound chicken, cut in serving pieces
1 tablespoon vegetable oil
1 cup chopped onion
4 tablespoons chile powder
salt and black pepper
2 cups canned hominy or corn kernels
For serving:
shredded lettuce or cabbage
sliced radishes
chopped scallions
chopped tomato
lime wedges

PREPARATION: 15 MINUTES
COOKING: 2 HOURS
SERVES: 4-6

2 Remove the chicken, ribs and pork. Discard the onion and strain the stock into a bowl. Dice the chicken, ribs and pork cubes, discarding any skin and bones.

3 Heat the oil and sauté the chopped onion until soft and golden. Stir in the chile powder, the reserved stock and salt and pepper to taste. Bring to the boil, then reduce the heat and add the hominy or corn kernels. Simmer gently for 15 minutes.

4 Add all the diced meat and simmer for a further 10 minutes. Serve piping hot topped with shredded lettuce or cabbage and sliced radishes, with scallions, chopped tomato and lime wedges.

61

PICADILLO

Beef stew

6 tablespoons shortening or bacon fat

1½ pounds ground beef

1 large onion, finely chopped

4 tablespoons red wine

3 tablespoons lime juice

2 tomatoes, skinned and chopped

2 small hot green chiles, chopped

½ cup stuffed green olives, sliced

2 green apples, peeled, cored
and chopped

3 tablespoons capers

½ cup raisins

2 large potatoes, peeled
and cut into small cubes

1 garlic clove, minced

½ teaspoon ground cumin

salt

½ cup chopped blanched almonds, toasted

2 Reduce the heat and add the wine and lime juice. Cook for 5 minutes and stir in the tomatoes, chiles, olives, apple, capers and raisins. Cover and simmer for 20 minutes.

3 Heat the remaining fat in another skillet. Fry the potatoes, garlic and cumin, turning occasionally, until evenly golden brown. Lower the heat and cook for 10-12 minutes until the potatoes are tender.

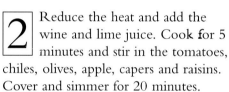

4 Add the potatoes to the meat mixture and cook gently for 5 minutes. Season to taste, transfer to a warm serving dish and sprinkle with the toasted almonds.

1 Heat half of the shortening or bacon fat in a heavy skillet. Add the beef and onion and cook over high heat, stirring constantly, until evenly browned.

PREPARATION: 15 MINUTES
COOKING: 35 MINUTES
SERVES: 4

TACOS
Fried stuffed tortillas

1 pound ground beef

½ cup chopped onion

½ cup chopped sweet green pepper

1 garlic clove, minced

1 teaspoon dried oregano

½ teaspoon hot paprika

¼ teaspoon ground cumin

¼ teaspoon dried hot red chile flakes

salt and black pepper

½ cup tomato paste

12 tortillas

oil for frying

For serving:

shredded lettuce

finely chopped tomatoes

grated Monterey Jack cheese

diced avocado

sour cream

salsa cruda (see page 111)

2 Add the onion, green pepper and garlic and cook, stirring occasionally, until softened. Stir in the herbs, spices and seasoning to taste.

3 Add the tomato paste and mix well. Cover and cook gently for 10 minutes, stirring occasionally.

1 Cook the ground beef in a skillet until brown and crumbly, stirring occasionally and breaking it up with a wooden spoon.

4 Place a little of the mixture on each tortilla and roll up. Secure with a wooden toothpick and fry quickly in a little oil until golden. Serve with the accompaniments.

PREPARATION: 15 MINUTES
COOKING: 30 MINUTES
SERVES: 4-6

CHILE VERDE

Green chile stew

1 Heat 3 tablespoons of the olive oil in a large heavy-based casserole and cook the stewing steak in batches, turning occasionally, over medium heat until lightly browned. Remove from the pan with a slotted spoon and keep warm. Pour off the meat juices and reserve.

2 Cut the sweet green peppers into 1-inch squares. Heat the remaining oil in the casserole and sauté the sweet green peppers and garlic over low heat for 5 minutes until the sweet peppers are cooked and tender.

PREPARATION: 10 MINUTES
COOKING: 2½ HOURS
SERVES: 4

3 Return the meat to the pan, and add the chiles, chopped tomatoes, brown sugar, cloves, cinnamon, cumin, lime juice and beef stock or wine. Bring to the boil, stirring continuously. Cover the casserole and cook in a preheated oven at 375° for 1¾ hours.

5 tablespoons olive oil
2 pounds stewing steak, cubed
3 sweet green peppers
3 garlic cloves, minced
4 fresh green chiles, seeded and finely sliced
1¾ cups canned chopped tomatoes
2 teaspoons brown sugar
¼ teaspoon ground cloves
¼ teaspoon ground cinnamon
2 teaspoons ground cumin
4 tablespoons lime juice
1½ cups beef stock or red wine
salt and freshly ground black pepper
3 tablespoons chopped cilantro

4 Remove the casserole from the oven, uncover and simmer gently on top of the stove for 20 minutes, or until the sauce has reduced and thickened. Season to taste with salt and freshly ground black pepper. Serve garnished with chopped cilantro.

TOSTADAS
Fried beef tortillas

8 tortillas

oil for frying

1 pound ground beef

2 red chiles, chopped

2 garlic cloves, minced

½ teaspoon ground cumin

½ cup tomato paste

¾ cup beef stock

1 tablespoon vinegar

2 tomatoes, skinned and chopped

For serving:

shredded lettuce

grated cheese

stoned black olives

2 Put the ground beef in a clean skillet and fry it gently in its own fat until it is cooked and browned, breaking it up as it cooks. Pour off and discard any excess fat.

3 Add the chopped chiles, garlic, cumin, tomato paste, beef stock and vinegar. Bring to the boil, stirring, and add the tomatoes. Reduce the heat and cook gently for 10-15 minutes until reduced and thickened.

4 Place a large spoonful of the meat mixture on each tostada (fried tortilla). Top with the shredded lettuce, grated cheese and the olives.

1 Fry the tortillas in about ¼ inch oil in a large skillet until they are crisp and golden – about 1 minute on each side. Keep warm while you make the topping.

PREPARATION: 20 MINUTES
COOKING: 25-30 MINUTES
SERVES: 4

CHORIZO ENCHILADAS

Meat-stuffed tortillas in chile sauce

1 pound ground pork

1 pound ground beef

1 tablespoon olive oil

1 large onion, finely chopped

2 garlic cloves, minced

1 tablespoon chile powder

$\frac{1}{2}$ teaspoon ground cumin

2 teaspoons dried oregano

pinch of salt

$\frac{1}{4}$ cup vinegar

1 cup beef stock

1$\frac{1}{2}$ cups red chile sauce
(see page 110)

oil for deep-frying

12 corn or flour tortillas

$\frac{2}{3}$ cup grated Monterey Jack cheese

To serve:

guacamole (see page 12)

sliced olives

2 Spread a little of the chile sauce over the base of 1 large or 2 small shallow baking dishes. Heat the oil in a deep skillet and fry the tortillas quickly on both sides – do not allow them to crisp up. Remove them with a slotted spoon and drain on paper towels.

3 Dip the tortillas into the chile sauce and put about 2 tablespoons of the meat filling down the center of each tortilla. Fold over and arrange in the baking dish(es).

4 Pour the remaining chile sauce over the top and scatter with the grated cheese. Bake in a preheated oven at 350° for 20–30 minutes until bubbling and golden brown. Serve with guacamole, garnished with olives.

1 Put the ground pork and beef in a skillet and cook in their own fat until browned and crumbly, breaking up the meat with a spoon. Add the oil, onion and garlic and cook until soft. Stir in the chile powder, cumin, oregano and salt, and then the vinegar and stock. Simmer for 10 minutes, or until the liquid has evaporated. Remove from the heat and cool.

PREPARATION: 40 MINUTES
COOKING: 20–30 MINUTES
SERVES: 6

EMPANADAS

Spicy pork turnovers

1 Make the filling: heat the oil in a skillet and sauté the onion and garlic until soft. Add the pork and cook, stirring, until lightly browned. Stir in the remaining ingredients and continue cooking until the excess liquid has evaporated. Remove from the heat and cool.

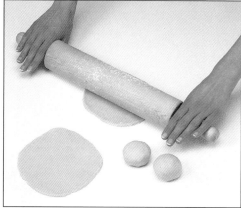

3 Divide the dough into 8 equal portions and roll them out on a lightly floured surface to make 6-inch diameter rounds.

2 cups all-purpose flour	
¼ teaspoon salt	
6 tablespoons shortening, diced	
4 tablespoons butter, diced	
6-8 tablespoons iced water	
beaten egg for glaze	
sesame seeds	
For the filling:	
1½ tablespoons oil	
½ cup chopped onion	
1 garlic clove, minced	
½ pound pork tenderloin, diced	
1 cup firmly packed shredded sweet potato	
4 juicy prunes, pitted and chopped	
½ cup unsweetened pineapple juice	
1 tablespoon tomato paste	
2 teaspoons chile powder	
salt	

2 Put the flour, salt and fats in a food processor, and process until the mixture resembles crumbs. Add enough iced water to make a soft dough. Shape into a ball and chill for 20-30 minutes.

PREPARATION: 30 MINUTES + CHILLING
COOKING: 35-40 MINUTES
SERVES: 4-6

4 Put one-eighth of the filling on each round. Dampen the edges and fold over to make half-moon shapes. Press the edges together and crimp with a fork. Place on a greased baking sheet, brush with beaten egg and sprinkle with sesame seeds. Bake in a preheated oven at 375° for 35-40 minutes.

73

BURRITOS DE PUERCO

Pork-stuffed tortillas

2 pounds boneless pork shoulder roast

1 tablespoon oil

salt

1½ cups meat stock

1 cup tomato paste

½ teaspoon grated orange peel

1 teaspoon dried hot red chile flakes

8 medium-sized flour tortillas

To serve:

guacamole, sour cream and refried beans

2 While the pork is cooking, make the sauce. Put the meat stock in a small saucepan with the tomato paste, orange peel and dried chile flakes. Bring to the boil, then reduce the heat and simmer gently for about 30 minutes until the sauce is reduced and thickened.

3 Remove any fat from the cooked pork and tear the meat into shreds, using a fork. Add to the sauce and heat through very gently over a low heat.

4 Wrap the flour tortillas in foil and heat through gently in a warm oven. Place a little of the pork mixture in the center of each tortilla and then roll up. Serve with guacamole, sour cream and refried beans.

1 Put the pork shoulder in a roasting pan and brush with a little oil. Sprinkle with salt, and cook in a preheated oven at 350° for about 1½ hours, or until crisp, golden and cooked through.

PREPARATION: 20 MINUTES
COOKING: 1½ HOURS
SERVES: 4

ARROZ VERDE

Green rice

1 Heat the shortening in a heavy skillet and stir in the rice. Cook, stirring frequently, until all the grains of rice are coated with fat and glistening.

2 Add the onion, garlic and tomatoes, and cook for 2 minutes. Add about 1½ cups of the broth, cover the skillet and simmer gently for about 25 minutes, or until the rice is tender and has absorbed all the liquid. Keep checking the rice and adding more stock as necessary. Season with salt and pepper.

PREPARATION: 10 MINUTES
COOKING: 30 MINUTES
SERVES: 4

3 Five minutes before the end of cooking time, heat the oil in another skillet, and stir-fry the pepper strips until they start to lose their crispness. However, they should still retain their bright green color.

4 Add the stir-fried pepper strips to the cooked rice, and stir in gently. Scatter with the sliced olives and serve immediately.

3 tablespoons vegetable shortening
³/4 cup long-grain rice
1 onion, finely chopped
1 garlic clove, minced
1³/4 cups drained and chopped canned tomatoes
1¹/2 cups chicken broth or stock
salt and pepper
2 tablespoons vegetable oil
2 sweet green peppers, seeded and cut into thin strips
²/3 cup pimiento-stuffed green olives, sliced

ARROZ A LA MEXICANA

Mexican rice

1 cup long-grain rice
4 tablespoons olive oil
2 garlic cloves, minced
1 small onion, grated
1 sweet red pepper, seeded and chopped
1 large tomato, skinned, seeded and chopped
1 tablespoon finely chopped fresh cilantro
1 tablespoon ground cumin
$2^1/_2$ –3 cups chicken or beef stock
salt and freshly ground black pepper

1 Place the rice in a sieve and rinse thoroughly with cold running water to remove any excess starch. Drain and tip the rice into a large bowl, and then cover with hot water. Leave to stand for 30 minutes.

3 Heat the oil in a heavy skillet and add the rice. Cook, stirring, over low heat until all the grains are well coated with oil, glistening and translucent. Add the garlic and onion and cook until they are transparent and the rice is golden.

2 Drain the rice thoroughly in a sieve, and then leave it in the sieve placed over a bowl for about 1 hour until it is really dry.

4 Add the sweet red pepper, tomato, cilantro, cumin and stock. Stir well, cover the pan and cook gently over very low heat for 20–30 minutes, until all the liquid has been absorbed and the grains of rice are tender and fluffy. Season with salt and pepper to taste and serve hot as an accompaniment to a main dish.

PREPARATION: 1½ HOURS
COOKING: 30–40 MINUTES
SERVES: 4

ARROZ CON MARISCOS
Rice with seafood

1 Prepare the seafood: wash and clean the octopus or squid and cut into rings. Cut the tentacles into small pieces. Wash and peel the shrimp. Cut the white fish into large chunks.

2 pounds mixed seafood, e.g. shrimp, octopus, squid, white fish, clams
2 tablespoons olive oil
1 large onion, chopped
2 garlic cloves, minced
1 cup long-grain rice
2½ –3 cups fish stock or clam juice
3 tomatoes, skinned and chopped
2 tablespoons chopped fresh parsley
salt and freshly ground black pepper
4 red or green chiles

To serve:

lime wedges and fresh cilantro

2 Heat the oil in a large skillet and sauté the onion and garlic until soft and golden. Add the rice and stir gently for a couple of minutes until all the grains are glistening with oil and slightly translucent.

PREPARATION: 15 MINUTES
COOKING: 45 MINUTES
SERVES: 4

3 Add some of the fish stock or clam juice together with the tomatoes and bring to the boil. Reduce the heat and simmer gently, adding more stock as and when necessary until all the liquid has been absorbed and the rice is tender. After 15 minutes, add the seafood. Stir in the parsley and season if necessary with salt and pepper when the rice is cooked.

4 Place a lightly oiled small skillet over medium to high heat and, when it is hot, add the chiles. Press them down hard with a spatula against the surface of the pan for about 1 minute each side until they change color. Take care that they do not burn. This helps to release their pungent aroma. Cut into thin strips and use as a garnish. Serve with lime wedges and cilantro.

FRIJOLES REFRITOS

Refried beans

| 1½ cups dried pinto beans |
| 4 garlic cloves, minced |
| 1 bay leaf |
| 4 tablespoons shortening or bacon fat |
| 1 cup chopped onion |
| salt and freshly ground black pepper |
| ½ cup grated Monterey Jack cheese |

1 Put the beans in a large bowl and cover with cold water. Leave to soak for at least 6 hours or, preferably, overnight. The following day, drain the beans and rinse them well under running cold water.

3 Drain the beans, reserving the cooking liquid. Discard the bay leaf. Mash the beans coarsely with a potato masher, or process in a blender or food processor, adding some of the reserved liquid as necessary until you achieve the desired consistency.

4 Melt the shortening or bacon fat in a skillet and sauté the onion, stirring, until soft. Add the beans and seasoning and mix well. Simmer until piping hot, continuing to mash and add more liquid as necessary. Serve hot, sprinkled with cheese, with the garnish of your choice, e.g. guacamole, sour cream, sliced avocado or salsa.

2 Put the beans in a large saucepan with the garlic and bay leaf. Cover with cold water and bring to the boil. Boil briskly for 10 minutes, then lower the heat to a bare simmer and cook gently for about 2 hours, until the beans are very tender.

PREPARATION: 20 MINUTES +
6 HOURS SOAKING
COOKING: 2½ HOURS
SERVES: 4-6

FAJITAS DE CHILES

Vegetable fajitas

2 tablespoons olive oil

2 large onions, thinly sliced

2 garlic cloves, minced

2 sweet red peppers, thinly sliced

2 sweet green peppers, thinly sliced

4 green chiles, seeded and thinly sliced

2 teaspoons chopped fresh oregano

$1/2$ pound button mushrooms, sliced

salt and freshly ground black pepper

To serve:

12 warmed tortillas

salsa and sour cream

2 Add the sliced sweet red and green peppers, chiles and oregano and stir well. Sauté gently for 10 more minutes, until cooked and tender.

3 Add the sliced button mushrooms and cook quickly for 1 more minute, stirring to mix thoroughly with the other vegetables. Season the vegetable mixture with salt and black pepper to taste.

4 To serve, spoon the sizzling hot vegetable mixture into the warmed tortillas and fold over or roll up. Serve very hot with salsa and plenty of sour cream.

1 Heat the olive oil in a large skillet and then gently sauté the sliced onions and garlic for about 5 minutes until they are soft and golden brown. They should be melting and almost caramelized.

PREPARATION: 15 MINUTES

COOKING: 16 MINUTES

SERVES: 4

CHILES RELLENOS

Mexican stuffed sweet peppers

1 Make a long slit in the side of each pepper and carefully scoop out the seeds without tearing the pepper. Trim the stalks if they are long. Stuff the sweet peppers with the prepared picadillo mixture.

6 large sweet green peppers
picadillo (see page 62)
2 eggs
salt and freshly ground black pepper
flour
oil for frying
salsa de jitomate (see page 110)
torn cilantro leaves to garnish

3 Dip the stuffed sweet peppers in some flour and then into the egg mixture. Heat some oil in a heavy-based skillet to a depth of $1/2$ inch, and fry the sweet peppers in batches over low heat, turning occasionally, until they are uniformly golden all over and the filling is sealed inside the egg coating. Drain on paper towels.

2 Separate the eggs, and beat the egg whites until they form stiff peaks. Beat the egg yolks and a little salt and pepper until lightly colored, and then gently fold in the beaten egg white.

4 Pour the salsa de jitomate into a large saucepan and stand the fried stuffed sweet peppers in the sauce. Simmer gently over low heat for 15-20 minutes. Serve in the sauce sprinkled with torn cilantro leaves.

PREPARATION: 25 MINUTES
COOKING: 15-20 MINUTES
SERVES: 6

CHIMICHANGA

Fried vegetable tortillas

2 tablespoons olive oil

1 small onion, chopped

1 sweet red pepper, seeded and diced

4 ounces button mushrooms, thinly sliced

$^1/_2$ pound small broccoli florets

2 tomatoes, skinned and chopped

2 red chiles, finely chopped

salt and freshly ground black pepper

$1^1/_2$ cups grated Monterey Jack cheese

8 flour tortillas (see page 10)

oil for deep-frying

To serve:

$^2/_3$ cup sour cream

guacamole (see page 12)

2 Remove the skillet from the heat, and mix the grated Monterey Jack cheese into the stir-fried vegetable mixture. Stir gently until the cheese melts.

1 Heat the olive oil in a large heavy-based skillet, and sauté the onion and red pepper until just tender but still slightly crisp. Add the mushrooms and broccoli florets, tomatoes and chiles and stir-fry over medium heat for 3-4 minutes. Season to taste with salt and pepper.

3 Divide the vegetable and cheese mixture into 8 portions and put one in the center of each of the tortillas. Roll up carefully, tucking in the edges at the sides so that the filling is completely sealed and cannot escape.

4 Deep-fry the tortillas, one or two at a time, in hot oil until crisp and golden, turning once during cooking. Drain on paper towels and serve the chimichanga with sour cream and guacamole.

PREPARATION: 20 MINUTES
COOKING: 15-20 MINUTES
SERVES: 4

GARBANZOS

Spicy garbanzo beans

2 cups dried garbanzo beans
1½ teaspoons salt
1 whole onion, peeled
6 bacon slices, chopped
2 onions, chopped
1 garlic clove, minced
1 sweet red pepper, seeded and chopped
¼ teaspoon ground black pepper
1 small dried hot red chile, crumbled
½ teaspoon dried oregano
1¼ cups skinned and chopped tomatoes
2 tablespoons tomato paste
6 tablespoons water or reserved bean liquid
2 tablespoons chopped fresh cilantro

2 Bring to the boil, and boil hard for 10 minutes. Reduce the heat and simmer, uncovered, for about 45 minutes, until the garbanzo beans are cooked and tender. Drain and reserve the cooking liquid.

3 Put the bacon in a skillet and fry until the fat starts to run out of the bacon. Add the onions, garlic and sweet red pepper and continue frying until soft. Stir in the remaining salt, the black pepper, chile, oregano, tomatoes, tomato paste and some of the reserved bean liquid.

1 Soak the garbanzo beans overnight in cold water. Drain and place in a saucepan with 1 teaspoon of the salt and the whole peeled onion. Cover with cold water.

4 Add the drained garbanzo beans and stir well. Simmer for 10 minutes, stirring occasionally. Serve hot, sprinkled with chopped fresh cilantro leaves.

PREPARATION: 1 HOUR +
SOAKING OVERNIGHT
COOKING: 30 MINUTES
SERVES: 4

VERDURAS CAPEADAS

Zucchini and cauliflower in batter

4 small zucchini

1 small head cauliflower, broken into florets

1½ cups grated Monterey Jack cheese

3 eggs, separated

salt and pepper

3 tablespoons flour

oil for deep-frying

To serve:

salsa de jitomate (see page 110)

1 Bring a large pan of salted water to the boil and tip in all the zucchini and cauliflower florets. Boil rapidly for a few minutes, until the vegetables are just tender but still crisp. Remove from the heat and drain well.

2 Make a slit along the side of each zucchini and scoop out a little of the flesh. Fill the hole with grated cheese. Stuff some of the grated cheese into the hollow of each cauliflower floret.

3 Beat the egg yolks lightly with the seasoning in a bowl. In another bowl, beat the egg whites until they are stiff and stand in peaks. Fold the beaten egg white gently into the yolks to make the batter.

4 Dip the cheese-filled vegetables in the flour and then into the batter. Heat the oil for deep-frying and fry the vegetables in batches until crisp and golden. Remove with a slotted spoon. Drain on paper towels. Serve hot with salsa de jitomate.

PREPARATION: 20 MINUTES
COOKING: 5-10 MINUTES
SERVES: 4

ENSALADA DE NOCHE BUENA

Christmas Eve salad

1 Prepare all the fruits and sprinkle with lemon or lime juice to prevent any discoloration.

2 Make the dressing: mix all the ingredients together and blend thoroughly, or put in a screwtop jar and shake vigorously until the sugar has completely dissolved.

3 Line a large bowl with lettuce leaves and arrange the sliced beets and fruit on top in attractive concentric circles, finishing with the banana. Sprinkle the dressing over the top of the salad.

1 green apple, peeled, cored and sliced
2 oranges, peeled and sliced
1/2 fresh pineapple, peeled, cored and sliced
1 large banana, sliced
1 large red apple, cored and sliced
1/2 cup lemon or lime juice
1 large lettuce
2 small cooked beets, peeled and sliced
1/4 cup unsalted roasted peanuts
seeds of 1/2 small pomegranate

For the dressing:

6 tablespoons olive oil
2 tablespoons lemon or lime juice
1 teaspoon sugar
1/4 teaspoon salt

4 Decorate the salad with the peanuts and pomegranate seeds and serve immediately.

PREPARATION: 25 MINUTES
SERVES: 4-6

FLAN

Mexican caramel custard

1 Put half of the sugar in a saucepan with a little water. Heat gently, stirring to dissolve the sugar. Boil briskly until the caramel turns golden. Pour a little into 6 dariole molds or custard cups, rotating the molds to cover them evenly.

3 Beat the egg and egg yolks together until light and frothy and then stir in the cooled milk.

2 Heat the milk in a heavy pan over low heat. Add the remaining sugar, salt, vanilla bean and cinnamon stick. Cook, stirring, for 2–3 minutes. Cool and remove the cinnamon stick and vanilla pod.

4 Strain the custard into the prepared molds. Stand in a roasting pan containing about 1 inch hot water and cook in a preheated oven at 350° for about 45 minutes, until set. Cool and chill. Unmold and serve decorated with cream and almonds.

¹/₂ cup sugar
2 cups milk
pinch of salt
1 vanilla bean
1 cinnamon stick
1 egg
3 egg yolks
For decoration:
¹/₃ cup heavy cream, whipped
blanched almonds, toasted and crushed

PREPARATION: 20 MINUTES
COOKING: 45 MINUTES
SERVES 6

BUNUELOS

Mexican puffed fritters

2 cups all-purpose flour

1 teaspoon baking soda

pinch of salt

1 tablespoon sugar

1 egg, well beaten

2 tablespoons melted shortening

$^1/_2$ cup milk

oil for deep-frying

For the syrup:

$1^1/_2$ cups water

4 tablespoons sherry

$^3/_4$ cup dark brown sugar

$^1/_2$ cinnamon stick

1 Sift the flour, baking soda and salt into a large mixing bowl. Stir in the sugar and mix in the beaten egg, shortening and enough milk to form a soft, but not too sticky, dough.

2 Divide the dough into 8–12 equal-sized pieces. With floured hands, shape each one into a ball. Cover with a sheet of plastic wrap and leave to stand for 30 minutes. Shape into flat cakes and make a shallow depression in the center of each one.

3 Heat the oil to 375° and deep-fry the cakes, a few at a time, until golden brown and puffy. Drain on paper towels.

4 Meanwhile, put all the syrup ingredients in a heavy saucepan and bring slowly to the boil, stirring. Simmer, stirring occasionally, for 20–30 minutes until the syrup thickens. Discard the cinnamon stick and serve the syrup with the bunuelos.

PREPARATION: 45 MINUTES
COOKING: 5 MINUTES
SERVES: 4-6

SOPAIPILLAS
Mexican fritters

1 Sift the flour, baking soda and salt into a bowl. Rub in the shortening and bind with enough lukewarm water to form a dough.

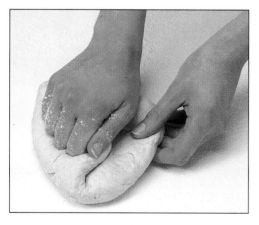

2 Knead the dough briefly until it is really smooth. Cover and then leave to stand at room temperature for about 20 minutes.

3 Roll out the dough on a lightly floured surface to ¼ inch thick. Trim the edges and cut the dough into 3-inch squares.

4 Heat the oil for deep-frying to 400°, and deep-fry the pieces of dough, two or three at a time, until they are puffed up and golden. Turn once so that they are evenly colored on both sides. Drain on paper towels. To serve, tear off a corner of each sopaipilla and pour in some honey flavored with cinnamon. Serve sprinkled with pomegranate seeds.

2 cups all-purpose flour
1 tablespoon baking soda
½ teaspoon salt
1 tablespoon shortening
⅔ –¾ cup lukewarm water
oil for deep-frying
honey warmed with a little ground cinnamon
To garnish:
fresh pomegranate seeds

PREPARATION: 35 MINUTES
COOKING: 5-10 MINUTES
SERVES: 4-6

CHURROS

Doughnuts

1 Cut the butter into pieces and put in a large saucepan with the water. Heat the water gently until the butter melts and then bring to a rolling boil.

2 Sift the flour at least twice and, as soon as the water boils, tip it into the pan all at once. Remove from the heat and beat in the flour. Continue beating until the mixture forms a ball and leaves the sides of the pan clean. Cool a little and then beat in the eggs, the extra yolk and the orange peel.

PREPARATION: 20 MINUTES
COOKING: 10 MINUTES
SERVES: 4–6

3 Spoon the mixture into a pastry bag fitted with a large star tip. Pipe it into 6-inch lengths, cutting between them. Heat the oil for deep-frying in a large saucepan.

²/₃ cup butter
1¹/₄ cups water
1¹/₄ cups all-purpose flour
3 eggs
1 egg yolk
grated peel of 1 orange
vegetable oil for deep-frying
1 tablespoon ground cinnamon
²/₃ cup sugar

4 Deep-fry the churros, a few at a time, until they are golden brown, turning them once. Remove and drain. Mix the cinnamon and sugar together and roll the churros in this mixture. Serve with some fresh fruit.

PAPAYAS Y PINA DIABLO

Papaya and pineapple flambé

1 Peel the papayas and scoop out the seeds. Cut the flesh into slices. Peel the pineapple and cut into thin slices. Remove the central core so that you are left with pineapple rings.

2 Melt the butter in a large heavy-based skillet and then stir in the sugar over low heat, stirring until it is thoroughly dissolved. Add the lime juice and grated peel.

3 Increase the heat slightly and let the sugary mixture bubble for a few minutes until thickened. Take care that it does not burn or turn to caramel. Add the papaya and pineapple and cook gently for 2 minutes. Sprinkle with ground cinnamon.

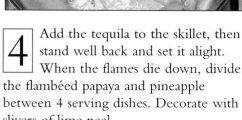

4 Add the tequila to the skillet, then stand well back and set it alight. When the flames die down, divide the flambéed papaya and pineapple between 4 serving dishes. Decorate with slivers of lime peel.

2 papayas
1 small pineapple
¼ cup butter
¼ cup soft brown sugar
juice and grated peel of 1 lime
½ teaspoon ground cinnamon
4 tablespoons tequila
To decorate:
slivers of lime peel

PREPARATION: 10 MINUTES
COOKING: 10 MINUTES
SERVES: 4-6

HELADO DE MANGO E PAPAYA

Swirled mango and papaya ice cream

1 cup milk
4 egg yolks
½ cup sugar
pinch of salt
1 cup fresh mango purée
1-2 teaspoons lime juice
1 cup heavy cream
⅔ cup fresh papaya purée
2 tablespoons white rum
confectioners' sugar to taste

2 Pour the custard into a bowl and cool. Stir in the mango purée and lime juice. Whip the cream until thick and beat lightly into the mango mixture. Pour into a rigid container, cover and freeze until just firm.

3 Mix together the papaya purée and rum, and then sweeten to taste with some confectioners' sugar.

1 Scald the milk in a heavy saucepan. Lightly beat the egg yolks with the sugar and salt until the mixture is pale. Gradually stir in the hot milk, then return to the saucepan and cook over low heat, stirring until the custard thickens. Do not allow to boil or the custard will curdle.

4 Put alternate spoonfuls of mango ice cream and the papaya mixture into a freezeproof container, and stir gently with a spoon to make a swirled effect. Cover and return to the freezer until firm. Soften at room temperature before serving.

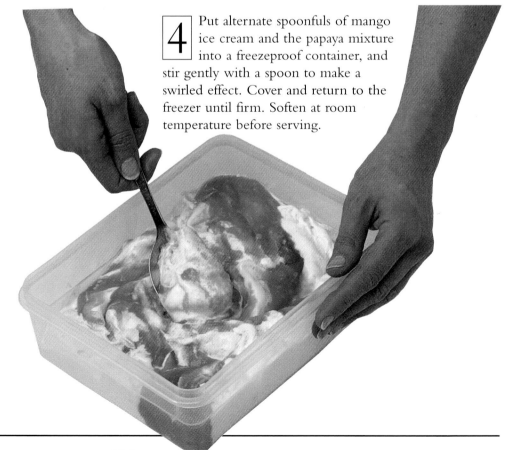

PREPARATION: 20 MINUTES
FREEZING: 4-5 HOURS
SERVES: 6-8

CAPIROTADA
Mexican bread pudding

1 cup water

1¹/₂ cups dark brown sugar

1¹/₂ teaspoons ground cinnamon

10 slices stale bread

¹/₄ cup butter

¹/₃ cup seedless white raisins

1 cup walnuts, chopped

1 cup cottage cheese

2 Remove the crusts from the bread and cut into small cubes. Melt the butter in a large skillet, add the bread cubes and fry gently until golden brown. Remove from the heat and stir in the syrup.

3 Add the seedless raisins, chopped walnuts and cottage cheese. Stir well and then simmer gently for a few minutes until all the ingredients are well blended.

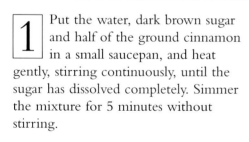

1 Put the water, dark brown sugar and half of the ground cinnamon in a small saucepan, and heat gently, stirring continuously, until the sugar has dissolved completely. Simmer the mixture for 5 minutes without stirring.

4 Transfer the mixture to a well-greased ovenproof dish and sprinkle with the remaining cinnamon. Cook in a preheated oven at 375° for 15–20 minutes until set and golden brown. Serve warm with cream.

PREPARATION: 20 MINUTES
COOKING: 15–20 MINUTES
SERVES: 4

TORTILLAS, SAUCES AND DRINKS

TORTILLAS
Corn tortillas

1½ cups masa harina
¾ cup water

Mix the masa harina and water together in a bowl with a fork to make a smooth dough. Add more water if necessary. Cover with a damp cloth and set aside for 15-20 minutes. Divide the dough into 12 portions and shape into balls. Flatten them in a tortilla press or by rolling them out with a rolling pin. Heat an ungreased griddle or cast-iron skillet until it is very hot and cook the tortillas, one at a time, for 1½-2 minutes on each side until they are lightly browned. Gently press out any bubbles that form while they are cooking. Wrap the cooked tortillas in a cloth and serve warm in a basket. Alternatively, use them for making tacos, tostadas etc. This quantity of dough makes 12 tortillas. These are the traditional corn tortillas with a slightly heavier texture than the ones made with wheat flour.

SALSA VERDE FRESCA
Fresh green tomato and chile sauce

1¼ cups canned tomatillos (Mexican green tomatoes), drained and chopped
1 small onion, finely chopped
1 garlic clove, minced
2 fresh green chiles, seeded and finely chopped
salt and freshly ground black pepper
pinch of sugar
few sprigs fresh cilantro, chopped

Put all the ingredients in a bowl and mix thoroughly until they are well blended. Alternatively, you can blend them in a food processor or blender for a smoother sauce – if so, add some chopped sweet green pepper to bulk it out. Serve with fish, meat and chicken dishes, moles and tacos. Makes about 1½ cups.

SALSA ROJA
Red chile sauce

5 small dried red chiles, crumbled
3 tablespoons boiling water
1¾ cups canned chopped tomatoes
4 tablespoons oil
2 onions, chopped
2 garlic cloves, minced
3 tablespoons tomato paste
1 teaspoon ground cumin
1 teaspoon ground cilantro
1½ tablespoons wine vinegar
1 teapoon sugar

Place the chiles and boiling water in a blender goblet or food processor. Drain the tomatoes, reserving the juice, and add the chopped tomatoes to the chiles. Blend until smooth and pour into a jug. Heat the oil in a small skillet and sauté the onions and garlic until soft. Stir in the blended tomato mixture, the reserved tomato juice, tomato paste, cumin, cilantro, vinegar and sugar. Cover and simmer for 10 minutes. Serve with tacos, enchiladas, meat, poultry and fish dishes. Makes about 1½ cups.

SALSA DE JITOMATE
Tomato sauce

2 tablespoons olive oil
1 medium onion, finely chopped
1 garlic clove, minced
4 large tomatoes, skinned and chopped
2 fresh green chiles, seeded and chopped
good pinch of sugar
salt and freshly ground black pepper
1 tablespoon chopped fresh cilantro

Heat the oil in a saucepan and add the onion and garlic. Sauté until tender and lightly golden. Blend the tomatoes and chiles in a blender or food processor, and add to the onion mixture with the sugar, salt and plenty of ground black pepper. Simmer gently for about 15 minutes, stirring occasionally until thickened. Stir in the chopped cilantro. Serve hot with meat and fish dishes. Makes about 1 cup.

SALSA CRUDA
Uncooked tomato chile sauce

1 pound large ripe tomatoes, skinned and chopped
2 fresh green chiles, seeded and finely chopped
1 onion, finely chopped
pinch of sugar
salt and freshly ground black pepper
few sprigs fresh cilantro, chopped

Put the tomatoes, chiles and onion in a bowl with the sugar. Season and stir in the cilantro. Makes about 2 cups.

CHILE CON QUESO
Chile and cheese dip

2 tablespoons oil
1/2 onion, chopped
2 garlic cloves, minced
1 cup canned green chiles, drained, seeded and chopped
3-4 tablespoons chopped seeded jalapeño chiles (optional)
1 cup chopped tomatoes,
6 tablespoons cream cheese
2 cups Monterey Jack cheese, grated
salt

Heat the oil in a heavy saucepan, and add the onion and garlic. Cook gently, stirring occasionally, until softened. Add the chiles and tomatoes, and cook until any excess liquid has evaporated, stirring frequently. Add the cheeses and cook very gently over low heat, stirring the mixture until the cheeses have melted into the dipping sauce. Season to taste. Serve warm as a dip. Serves 4.

CHOCOLATE MEXICANO
Mexican hot chocolate

2 1/2 cups milk
4 squares semisweet dark chocolate, grated
3 tablespoons sugar
1/2 teaspoon ground cinnamon
2-3 drops vanilla extract
pinch of ground cloves

Put the milk and grated chocolate in a medium-sized saucepan, and add the sugar, cinnamon, vanilla extract and cloves. Place the pan over moderate heat and stir constantly until the chocolate and milk are well blended and the sugar has dissolved. Bring to the boil, and then beat with a whisk or a traditional wooden *molinillo* (Mexican chocolate whisk) until frothy. Serve in cups or mugs sprinkled with a little ground cinnamon, if wished. Serves 3-4.

MARGARITA
Mexican tequila cocktail

2 tablespoons freshly squeezed lime juice
coarsely ground salt
2 tablespoons white tequila
1 tablespoon curacao or Triple Sec
ice cubes or crushed ice

Put 2 teaspoons of the lime juice in a shallow container and dip the rim of the cocktail glass in it. Next dip the rim of the glass into a saucer of coarsely ground salt. Mix the tequila with the curacao or Triple Sec and the remaining lime juice. Pour into the prepared glass and serve iced. Add a twist of lime peel if wished. **Note:** for an iced margarita, blend the tequila, lime juice and curacao or Triple Sec with plenty of crushed ice in a blender until slushy. Serve in the prepared frosted glass.

AGUA DE LIMON
Fresh lime or lemon drink

4 1/2 cups water
1/2 cup sugar
1 whole lime or lemon
juice of 3 limes or lemons
ice cubes or crushed ice

Pour half the water into a blender with the sugar and 1 whole lime or lemon, quartered. Add the squeezed lime or lemon juice, and blend until thoroughly mixed and the lime or lemon peel has been whizzed into tiny green or yellow specks in the drink. Strain into a jug containing the remaining water and mix well. Serve with ice cubes or crushed ice and a twist of lime or lemon peel. Serves 4-6.

INDEX